ORANGE COUNTY
THEN & NOW

Capistrano Mission Depot

ORANGE COUNTY THEN & NOW

DORIS I. WALKER

THUNDER BAY
P · R · E · S · S
San Diego, California

Thunder Bay Press
An imprint of the Advantage Publishers Group
5880 Oberlin Drive, San Diego, CA 92121-4794
www.thunderbaybooks.com

Produced by Salamander Books,
an imprint of the Anova Books Company Ltd,
151 Freston Road, London W10 6TH, U.K.

© 2006 Anova Books Company Ltd

All notations of errors or omissions should be addressed to Thunder Bay Press,
Editorial Department, at the above address. All other correspondence (author
inquiries, permissions) concerning the content of this book should be addressed to
Salamander, Anova Books, 151 Freston Road, London W10 6TH, U.K.

ISBN-13: 978-1-59223-599-5
ISBN-10: 1-59223-599-9

Library of Congress Cataloging-in-Publication Data available upon request.

1 2 3 4 5 10 09 08 07 06

Printed in China

ACKNOWLEDGMENTS

My deep appreciation goes to two historians who reviewed my text and offered
quality suggestions. They are Orange County's Archivist, Phil Brigandi, who knows
so many finite answers or where to find them, and my fellow Orange County
Historical Commissioner, Don Dobmeier, a living encyclopedia of Orange County
facts. Thanks go to other members of our Historical Commission, which coordinates
countywide historical sites and programs. The First American Corporation is
appreciated for maintaining its immense photo archives, as is Bob Blankman, who
marshals the collection. To local history librarians, historical societies, and authors of
city histories, I'm so glad you were there. Hearty hugs to my husband, Jack P. Smith,
for his support along the way, his pride in my work, and his thoughtful final proofing
of my text.

PICTURE ACKNOWLEDGMENTS

The publisher wishes to thank the following for kindly supplying the photographs
that appear in this book:

Then photographs:
Anaheim Public Library: p48, p74, p92.
Don Dobmeier Collection: p80, p118.
Doris Walker Collection: p6, p14, p16, p50, p114, p116, p120, p128, p130, p132,
p134, p134 (inset), p136.
Esther Cramer Collection: p68, p70.
First American Corporation Collection: p6 (inset), p12, p20, p22, p22 (inset), p24,
p28, p28 (inset) p30, p32, p34, p36, p38 (inset), p40, p44, p46, p54, p56, p58, p60,
p62, p64, p66, p72, p74, p76, p78, p82, p84, p86, p88, p94, p96, p98, p100, p102,
p104, p106, p108, p110, p112, p122, p124, p126, p138, p140, p142.
© Getty Images/Hulton Archive: p52.
Heritage Hill Historical Park: p18.
Los Alamitos Museum Association: p90.
Phil Brigandi Collection: p42.
San Juan Capistrano Historical Society Collection: p8, p10.
Steve Donaldson Collection: p38.
Tustin Area Historical Society: p24, p26 (inset).

Now photographs:
All Now photographs © Simon Clay (Anova Books Image Library) except ©
Ambient Images Inc. / Alamy p53 and © Fred Prouser / Reuters / Corbis p51.

Anova Books Group Ltd is committed to respecting the intellectual property rights
of others. We have therefore taken all reasonable efforts to ensure that the
reproduction of all content on these pages is done with the full consent of copyright
owners. If you are aware of any unintentional omissions, please contact the company
directly so that any necessary corrections may be made for future editions.

INTRODUCTION

It matured from a group of native villages to an isolated mission outpost, then a cluster of ranches, to a scattering of villages and landings, and finally to a complex of thirty-four independent cities. That is the story of Orange County, California, in a sentence. The flow of human history through this county began at the rivers and creeks that moved water from the mountains to the seashore. On the banks of these watercourses, the first people lived off the land that was, like them, nourished only by nature. The Spanish settlement's first significant structure, Mission San Juan Capistrano, dating from 1776, defines the relatively short extent of our written history.

Orange is the only county in Southern California not named for its major city. San Diego, Los Angeles, Ventura, Santa Barbara, Riverside, and San Bernardino are all big cities that gave their names to their counties. Unlike a large city circled by suburbs, whose history must be included in each of its satellite settlements' stories, Orange County's history is an anthology of independent stories. Similar things may have happened in them, but the details are different. When you turn the pages of this book, you will sense how communities evolved individually, many for wholly different reasons: Brea as an oil town; Laguna Beach as an artists' community. As a metropolitan area without a central core city, Orange County is like a modern theme park, where one must travel around to experience all the attractions before understanding the overall plan. There are, after all, world-class examples to follow—namely Disneyland and Knott's Berry Farm.

This book first follows the mission path—El Camino Real—that became the major thoroughfare through Southern California. That earthen path became a graded road, then a concrete highway, now a major freeway. Then our photo journey moves across the northern tier of Orange County cities, last traveling down the coast highway. This gives the reader a relative parallel to the chronology of local history here.

There were many significant influences that brought towns into being. The major ones were agricultural crops as diverse as celery or sugar beet, grapes or oranges, walnuts or lima beans. Then there were railroads, oil strikes, freeways, and always people arriving from elsewhere to seek a better job or a better life, embracing the outstanding location and climate waiting for them south of Los Angeles.

There were high points when individuals or groups were added to the scene: rail, oil, and farm workers as those industries needed them; World War II veterans in the 1950s; Vietnam refugees in the 1970s; and since then scientific workers in aerospace, computer, and biomedical fields. Orange County has come to mean groups of individuals working toward their own destinies while living comfortably with their neighbors and benefiting from their union.

Today we have thirty-four city halls and thirty-four mayors. There are even more settlements that didn't make it to cityhood. Almost all of these have had one or more dynamic individuals behind their formation, but their dreams didn't all come true. Sometimes, someone else stepped in and finished the dream for them.

Orange County was born after twenty years of attempts to separate from Los Angeles County, which spoke against the split in the determining state legislature. Representatives from San Francisco, however, urged the division, glad to bring rival Los Angeles down in size. By 1888, Anaheim's population had risen above 1,000, having grown out of the boundaries of its original German wine-producing colony. Newcomer Santa Ana, by contrast, was booming with more than triple the people: 3,500. Orange was the third and smallest city already incorporated. Fullerton and Buena Park were embryo settlements. Counting all the farm and ranch folks and those residing at the ocean landings, swamps, and mission town, the total population of the proposed county was little more than 14,000 citizens, 70 percent of them living on farms or ranches. The chunk of land decided on was about 789 square miles, twice as long as wide. There were four railroad lines and fifteen miles of street railways—but no paved roads. There were some railroad tracks, but trains ran infrequently. Remnants of little boomtowns were withering away. Why the name Orange County was chosen, though, is still a local controversy. The citrus fruit was not yet a major agricultural crop during the years the communities were trying to break away and form their own county.

Once the break from Los Angeles became official in 1889, everyone went back to work. More people came, and the farms flourished. Eventually, Orange County would become famous for producing the very crop for which it had been so appropriately—but prematurely—named. That name, though, was destined to outlive the orange groves that would be sacrificed in the cause of development.

Orange County reveals its dominant heritage in its Spanish architecture and street names. Western dress and rodeos mark its major rancho role in raising cattle. There are annual festivals honoring swallows and whales; art pageants and tall ships' regattas; and Asian, Hispanic, international, and hometown heritage celebrations. While Orange County covers only one half of one percent of the land in California, it now has about 12 percent of that state's population and has more inhabitants than do twenty other states. Fifty years ago, orange trees outnumbered people here. Now there are more than three million people who call it home, but there are very few orange trees except in private yards. There are, of course, many other amenities to make up for that deficit.

Native people populated the Southern California coast for centuries before European explorers arrived to found a chain of Christian missions. The one established as Mission San Juan Capistrano in 1776 became the cradle of Orange County's Spanish-textured history. By 1806, the settlement was flourishing as an agricultural and ranching enterprise. Its major structure was the grandest stone building west of the Mississippi River. However, its stature was greatly diminished by an earthquake only six years later; its bell tower fell and left the church in ruins. A village of adobe homes beside the mission continued to house the native descendants. In the inset photo, village women survey the badly damaged ruins little more than a century after the mission was founded. Restoration efforts during the 1920s brought back some of the missing links. The protective adobe wall, pictured here, was added in 1917—even before the highway it faced was paved.

Of California's twenty-one Spanish missions, San Juan Capistrano is known as the "Jewel," famous for its beautiful grounds and the legendary cliff swallows, which are said to return to their nesting sites in the Capistrano Valley each spring. More jewels are seen in the year-round colorful flower gardens that surround fountains within the complex. Over the past few decades, restoration work has brought back to life the mission's west wing as well as its romantic corridor arches and work areas, which include an iron smelter, wine and olive presses, and a vat where cattle hides were treated to trade with merchant ships. Museum rooms recall the early days, as do living-history docents who take on historical roles. Educational programs acquaint students with the early rural lifestyle, such as adobe brick making. Mission San Juan Capistrano attracts more than half a million visitors a year, making it one of Orange County's most popular attractions.

By the 1890s, visitors enjoyed posing for photographs among the romantic ruins of Mission San Juan Capistrano's Great Stone Church. Moves were then being made to restore the historic buildings. The Landmarks Club of Los Angeles visited the site—its members removed four hundred tons of debris and repaired wall damage throughout the complex. They also reroofed the buildings within the main quadrangle. After more than a century of deterioration had weakened the mission's complex structures, a stabilization project was continued under the custodianship of Father St. John O'Sullivan in the 1920s, until his death in 1933. This included the installation of a "golden" altar in the Serra Chapel, so named because it is the only sanctuary still standing in California where the mission's founder, Father Junipero Serra, conducted mass.

Mission San Juan Capistrano's Great Stone Church, destroyed so suddenly 175 years before, has received careful attention in a stabilization program that began in 1987—one of the largest preservation projects in California. Major reconstruction to give this National Historic Landmark seismic strength was continued throughout recent decades. The ongoing stabilization using state-of-the-art engineering processes included repair of the decorative ribs of the sanctuary and part of the nave of the Great Stone Church. The final major step in preserving the church was stabilization of the sanctuary dome, which was found to be brick and not stone as previously thought. The Serra Chapel, including its golden altar, is now being stabilized and restored. Funding for this ongoing preservation has come from both private and government funds.

In 1894, the Santa Fe Railway constructed what would become known as one of the most outstanding examples of Mission Revival architecture in the West—a landmark rail depot on the California frontier. Tiny, isolated San Juan Capistrano, at the midpoint between Los Angeles and San Diego, had awaited the 1888 rail connection with excitement. Even before the depot was built, groups of residents gathered to view each smoky steam engine that stopped or passed through town. A race had developed between the Southern Pacific and the Santa Fe to connect Southern California's two biggest cities. The north-south challenge was the need to cross the vast private Irvine Ranch in Orange County to make the connection. The Santa Fe Railway finally won the right to construct its line, and Capistrano became an important stop.

The historic domed Capistrano Depot has lost its white stucco exterior, revealing the original red bricks beneath it. It has been called "the finest depot on the Santa Fe system." The Capistrano Depot restaurant now offers travelers dining areas inside the station, outside on the patio, and in vintage passenger rail cars. An authentic caboose is parked behind it. The original garden square is now an outdoor train waiting area beside a multistory parking garage for commuters. A garden of native California plants forms a dramatic transition across the tracks—from modern Amtrak Surf Line and Metrolink commuter trains to Los Rios Street. Some of the nearby homes are almost as old as the mission itself. Some were made of adobe bricks, some of board-and-batten construction. These homes form the oldest residential community in California, Los Rios National Historic Neighborhood.

By the 1920s, El Camino Real (the mission trail) was a paved street with curbs when it entered San Juan Capistrano. The town had water pipes and sewers as well as electricity. At the far right, looking south from the mission, is Hotel Capistrano, completed in 1920 with bell towers of its own. It also had its own restaurant and gift shop. In 1919, the two-towered Romer and Kelly building replaced the Woodmen's Hall, which was moved toward the

depot and the citrus packing house. Kelly's General Store was on the left, as was White Garage, offering the only automotive repair service in the thirty miles between Tustin and San Clemente. Agriculture would continue to surround the old town center until the 1950s. However, the tourist trade was becoming the mission town's mainstay. Incorporation would wait until 1961, when its population was still barely 1,300.

Modern San Juan Capistrano has preserved much of its Spanish architecture in the downtown area. Hotel Capistrano is gone, but the twin-towered building, since renamed the Provincial Building, still stands erect on the right. It serves as offices for small businesses. Beyond it is a two-story adobe from 1841, the Garcia Adobe, which was the old French Hotel and now holds shops. The left side of this main street, looking south, features the Swallow's Inn, a landmark cowboy bar with movie credits. Half a block beyond is the Old Barn Antiques Mall, which encompasses several old buildings. At the far left center lies the historic brick Judge Egan home of 1883. Once known as Harmony Hall, it has been a restaurant, an art gallery, and is now a home interiors shop.

In the mid-1800s, the land between the Pacific Ocean and the Santa Ana Mountains that would become Orange County before the end of the century had only one town—San Juan Capistrano. Cattle ranches stretched over the rest of the terrain, ranging in size from 1,000 to 50,000 acres. Many thousands of long-horned cattle moved freely through these unfenced parcels. They were tended by cowboys who moved around just as freely, with mobile cow camps like this one pictured in the South County during the 1880s. Horses pulled the chuck wagons (seen behind the horse) as well as wagons full of equipment and tents (at left). The cattle depended on the native grasses that grew wild and the creeks that flowed naturally. Land grants were distributed by the Spanish and, later, Mexican officials to individuals with political stature.

By the end of the twentieth century, most of Orange County's land had been subdivided for housing tracts, businesses, and shopping complexes—or protected in natural parks and preserves. While Ranchos Trabuco and Mission Viejo today form the cities of Mission Viejo, Rancho Santa Margarita, and other communities, only one sizable herd of cattle remains—on Rancho Mission Viejo. Instead, the 17.4 square miles that form today's city of Mission Viejo are home to more than 93,000 residents within a planned community whose acreage also includes sports parks, golf courses, open spaces, and a man-made lake. Recreational Lake Mission Viejo, built in Oso Creek Canyon in the 1970s, has as its natural basin what had once been a large bean and barley farm, now resting beneath the 124-acre lake.

The first Europeans to cross Orange County in 1769 followed Indian trails through natural brush below the foothills of the Santa Ana Mountains. As the Portolá expedition passed through the rugged terrain, they camped in what would become the Capistrano Valley, then moved on to Trabuco Mesa. *Trabuco* is Spanish for a blunderbuss firearm; the name marked the loss of one in this rugged but peaceful countryside. Rancho Trabuco had been granted in 1841 to Santiago Arguello, who built an adobe home there for himself, his wife, and their twenty-two children. Cattle, sheep, and horses were not the only creatures on the Trabuco, as this lone 1920s automobile indicates. The bricks of native soil, straw, and oil were no match for even Southern California's mild weather, as wind and rain dissolved them until only this ruin remained.

Mule deer, coyotes, bobcats, and grizzly bears made their home on this open mesa, as did game birds (and hunters). There were even California condors soaring over the landscape. During the 1870s, 20,000 sheep grazed around the disappearing adobe. Today, the scene retains its natural setting as part of Orange County's O'Neill Regional Park. In 1948 the Richard O'Neill family, owners of Rancho Trabuco and Rancho Mission Viejo, gave Orange County a 278-acre section in Trabuco Canyon, which became the initial phase of

O'Neill Regional Park. Additional gifts and purchases have brought the current acreage of the park to more than 3,000 acres. In 1966 Rancho Mission Viejo placed a protective cover over the ruin; a blessing from Mission San Juan Capistrano hopefully assured its perpetual place in open space. A plaque near the site marks the 1769 Portolá campsite, close to the Tijeras Creek Golf Club in the city of Rancho Santa Margarita.

During the 1840s, Jose Serrano received two grants giving him a ranch of more than 10,000 acres—Cañada de Los Alisos (canyon of the sycamores). Serrano, who had served as judge of the plains at Los Angeles, would build five adobes on his ranch over time. This is the only one that survives, pictured in 1935. Recurring droughts and floods in the 1860s wiped out the herds of cattle the family raised and caused hardship for ranchers throughout the region. Serrano was forced to sell his vast property, and Englishman Dwight Whiting bought most of the ranch, including this adobe, in 1884. He and his family lived there while he was founding the town of Aliso City around it. It was later called El Toro, and when incorporated in 1991, it became Lake Forest. Whiting's son, George, restored and further improved the adobe as his family home.

It was once a long way from this 1863 Serrano adobe to any other building. However, this structure, though never straying from its original foundation, drew a landmark village to its side. A street named Serrano Road came by. Then three buildings of early El Toro moved in to join the adobe as parts of Heritage Hill Historical Park. All four structures are furnished as they were in their time. The 1890 one-room schoolhouse held eight grades until 1914. In its second life, it became St. Anthony's Catholic Church until 1968. It was moved to the "Hill," an Orange County historical park, in 1976. St. George's Episcopal Mission, built in 1891, served the "gentlemen fruit farmers" who were El Toro residents. The only remaining vintage ranch house in El Toro, built on the Harvey Bennett citrus ranch in 1908, was also moved to Heritage Hill. All four buildings are open to the public and are used for special events.

This was the Irvine Ranch's headquarters in the late 1800s. The heavy horsepower was rounded up in neat rows to pose with the main barns, and a vintage wagon was filled with the many agricultural products that were grown on this expanse. Selling merchandise to gold rush miners made Irish immigrant James Irvine's fortune. It enabled him to invest in vast stretches of Orange County ranch land at about a dollar and a half an acre in the 1870s.

He amassed 108,000 acres stretching from the Pacific Ocean to the Santa Ana Mountains. Major crops were phased in and out—hay and grain, citrus and walnuts, and field crops—as were cattle and sheep. The Irvine family home was built at the edge, and the agricultural headquarters that had started there developed around it. No "gentleman farmer," James Irvine II set about making ranching his life's work.

Fifteen acres of the Irvine Ranch agricultural headquarters have been preserved as Irvine Ranch Headquarters Historic Park. Besides this "driving barn," the photo shows the scale house and the still-operative scale that was used to weigh vehicles and their agricultural cargoes. In addition to barns, the park will include the ranch bunkhouse, the mess hall, and several houses from foreman's row. The driving barn sheltered mules, horses, carriages, heavy equipment, feed—and later, automobiles. The park will have sample plantings of crops, including a lemon orchard. Irvine Ranch was one of the largest farms in California, and by 1894 it had taken on corporate structure. The exterior of the Irvine family home will be re-created to hold an Orange County library branch within the park. From the Irvine Ranch was developed the nation's largest master-planned urban complex, which became the city of Irvine in 1971.

After railroad tracks crossed the Irvine Ranch in 1887, a barley warehouse to store tenant farmers' crops was built in 1895; then a second warehouse was added. These served to store sacks of lima and garbanzo beans, black-eyed peas, barley, and oats. A third building was necessary within five years, and eventually a hotel and houses were built. A school, boarding house, post office, and blacksmith shop were added to accommodate seasonal warehouse workers and their families. Lima bean production soared during World War I. Its beanfield, of an estimated 50,000 acres, made Irvine Ranch one of the largest lima bean producers in the world. Thirty-two 35-foot-tall honeycomb concrete silos were built, capable of holding 16 million pounds of beans and barley. As the orange crop peaked, a packing house was needed.

In 1977, the Irvine Historical Society, working with the City of Irvine, became the watchdog of historical structures remaining on the ranch. Necessary widening of Sand Canyon Avenue for the Interstate 5 freeway threatened this site, but positive pressure led to the six-and-a-half-acre adaptive restoration of Old Town Irvine. The focal point is the warehouse-silo complex—now part of the attractive La Quinta Motor Inn. The 1895 warehouse, the 1949 silos, and the 1908 blacksmith shop qualified for the National Register of Historic Places. The hexagonal concrete silos now hold 98 of the motel's 150 rooms. Half the rooms are hexagons, the rest half-hexagons, with windows and doorways cut through the thick concrete walls. The wooden warehouse, with its funky corrugated tin siding, has become Tijuana's Restaurant, with the longest bar in Orange County. The blacksmith shop is now a restaurant; its walls and ceiling display old tools of that trade.

As the railroad was about to invade small-town life, a business boom began in the 1880s. Shareholders of the Tustin Land and Improvement Company opened the Bank of Tustin in 1888. Confidently, they built this two-story edifice at the crossroads of town, at what is now El Camino Real and Main Street. The bank also helped finance the Tustin Hotel, a three-story Victorian frame building with forty guest rooms, a block away. The inset photo shows its grand opening. The bank and the hotel were both stops on the horsecar trolley line. This Santa Ana, Orange, and Tustin Street Railway was the area's first public transportation, but service to Tustin ended not long after this photo was taken in 1890. When the Santa Fe Railway won the right-of-way through the Irvine Ranch, it too favored Santa Ana, and Tustin folks had to hitch a horse to get to the train. The hotel with no tourists was converted to a rooming house, and it closed for good in 1902.

After the 1933 Long Beach earthquake, building codes were changed throughout the county and state. The dramatic bank turret that overhung the sidewalk and all its decorative gingerbread-house features were removed as a safety precaution for the future. The hotel and the trolley were gone forever. Three hitching posts were added as a historic touch at the corner where the bank had stood, until it was razed in the 1960s. Founder Columbus

Tustin divided his acreage into 300-square-foot blocks, naming the east-west streets First, Second, Third, and Fourth. The north and south streets were A, B, C, and D. Now Fourth is Irvine Boulevard, and D Street is El Camino Real. This area is proudly called Old Town Tustin, where the small-town identity of the city is being preserved.

In 1914, when "grammar school" included the first eight grades, Tustin Grammar School was built on C Street at Second. It had a classroom for each grade and a large auditorium on the first floor, a wood shop for boys, a home economics room for girls, and shower rooms in the basement. The Reading Room became the town's public library in 1924. When the 1933 earthquake seriously damaged the school, the library was moved to a small room in the Bank of Tustin building. The students had classes in stores and churches during repairs. The postmistress, also a library board member, got her husband to build shelves for books. In 1938 she was able to have the library moved to a former drugstore on Main Street. That time, students in the high school wood-shop class built the shelves, magazine racks, tables, and benches.

By the time the earliest grammar school students had become senior citizens, the site no longer held a school. In 1990, the Tustin Area Senior Center was built on C Street at Second. It has classrooms, but instead of an auditorium, there are meeting rooms; instead of a wood shop, there are exercise facilities. The landmark specimen of Tustin's official tree, the red-flowering eucalyptus, is growing on C Street opposite the senior center. Meanwhile, the city library got its own building in 1958, and it was enlarged in 1963. Since the civic center was completed in 1976, the county branch library has been housed in it. Now that library is, in turn, being rebuilt and enlarged.

The 1941 attack on Pearl Harbor alerted the U.S. Navy of the need to fortify the coasts of America with fragile blimps that could quietly patrol for enemy submarines. Since each K-class blimp was as long as a football field, abundant land was needed for hangars. The Navy chose and purchased about 1,500 acres of James Irvine's vast bean fields. Steel was reserved for other military needs, so the two massive hangars—each to house six blimps—were built of wood. First, concrete foundations were poured. Tiered scaffolds fourteen stories high, pictured here, rode on flatbed railcars running the 1,088-foot length of the hangars to erect fifty-one trusses for each 178-foot-high structure. A heavy rainstorm and a Santa Ana windstorm played havoc with construction. However, the establishment known as the U.S. Navy Lighter-Than-Air Base, Santa Ana, was commissioned by the end of 1942. Navy pilots flew the blimps to patrol for submarines, monitor convoys, and aid in sea rescues. The inset shows one of the blimps over the air base chapel.

After World War II, the blimps left the local scene. In the 1950s, the base was recommissioned as Marine Corps Air Station, Tustin. This time the hangars housed CH-53 helicopters, with each hangar capable of holding as many as one hundred. In 1974, the hangars and their coastal counterparts were placed on the National Register of Historic Places as "the largest unsupported wooden structures in the world." The military base was closed permanently in 1999.

Seen here is one of the stories-high hangar doors. For years the Irvine Ranch had grazed flocks of sheep around the massive empty structures. Now the hangars have come to another turning point in their colorful career. The land beneath them has become more valuable than their international status, as urbanization has reached them from all directions. Their fate, whether it be housing museums or other worthwhile endeavors, is being evaluated.

In 1897, rancher James Irvine II offered the new Orange County 160 acres of his land in Santiago Canyon for a public park. The site was the wooded area early residents were already enjoying, calling it the "Picnic Grounds." It became the first designated county park in California. In 1898 a dramatic arch was erected at the entrance. Set in a grove of centuries-old live oaks and sycamores, the sylvan park attracted residents and visitors like these early motorists, photographed at the entrance sign in the late 1920s. Additional tree species from around the world were added to the park, making it a literal arboretum. It was also popular as a Hollywood movie set. In one film, the Irvine Ranch traded the use of three hundred horses for the movie crew's help in their roundup. By 1929, the expanse became known as Irvine Park.

Today Orange County has an enviable estate of 32,000 acres of regional parks. They offer natural beauty and scenic contrast, showing visitors how the land once was. The park is now officially Irvine Regional Park, encompassing 477 acres. In 1997, the centennial year of Irvine's first gift, the old sign was replaced with an updated Centennial Arch. At the same time, an eight-foot bronze statue of the donor, James Irvine II, was dedicated. Standing tall among the trees, he is portrayed in his favorite sport, hunting, with his dogs sharing the spotlight. The statue is called *Winds of Change*. Other attractions of the park added in the last century include the Orange County Zoo, featuring native animals of the canyon, and a miniature train that carries visitors who choose to ride rather than hike the many miles of trails.

In 1889, the year that Santa Ana was successful in a contentious election to make it the official county seat, its downtown looked like this. The city's population was 3,600, and it had already been incorporated as a city, as had Anaheim and Orange. Santa Ana's unpaved Fourth Street at Main held the track of the horse-drawn trolley that also served Tustin and Orange. Looking west, the tallest structure is the redbrick-faced First National Bank of Santa Ana, which would be a landmark for more than a century. Down the block, in the center of the photo, is the multisteepled Brunswick Hotel. Pushcarts and horse-drawn buggies constitute the nonfoot traffic. Two important Santa Ana families are represented by businesses on the right: Swanner's Grocery and McFadden's Hardware.

Fourth Street west of Main in Santa Ana is now lined with shops and offices. The dominant old building at the center of this photo is Rankin's Department Store, built in 1917. It became the place to shop in Orange County during the 1930s and 1940s. Rankin's was also one of the few places for respectable ladies to work in downtown Santa Ana, as was the county courthouse. The landmark downtown building stands on the far left: the third W. H. Spurgeon Building, whose stylish clock tower has made up for the one that never graced the courthouse, was built in 1917. The dominant modern building behind the holiday star is the tallest building in today's Santa Ana, the Ronald Reagan Federal Building and U.S. Courthouse, built in 1999 at 411 West Fourth Street. This ten-story, travertine-faced structure has many aesthetic touches, including statuary. Situated on a four-acre site, it contains fourteen courtrooms. The award-winning design has become a catalyst in the major revitalization of downtown Santa Ana.

Orange County's headquarter offices were located in two downtown store buildings for more than a decade before this impressive courthouse was completed in 1901. It was constructed of brick and steel, with a facing of gray Temecula granite and red Arizona sandstone. The three-story Richardsonian Romanesque–style building held court on a lot purchased from the founder of Santa Ana, William Spurgeon, who had mapped out the downtown area and reserved this site for a courthouse long before the county became a reality in 1889. The building opened with a celebration that included a "grand illumination," demonstrating its advanced dual electric and gas lighting system. The fancy cupola was initially intended to hold a clock, which was then eliminated to cut expenses. The courthouse would go on to become the county's hall of justice until the end of 1968. It is listed on the National Register of Historic Places. William Spurgeon became a charter member of the Orange County board of supervisors.

The Old Orange County Courthouse is now the oldest existing courthouse in Southern California. Its main courtroom, judges' chambers, jury room, and court reporter's office have all been faithfully restored. After the 1933 earthquake damaged the roof gables and granite steps, the cupola was removed and has never been replaced. Instead of trials, the courthouse now holds the Orange County Archives, offices of the Orange County Historical Commission, the marriage license office, and a museum and gallery. The California State Supreme Court held a regular session in the old courtroom during the building's centennial year, 2001. It has played a part in many movies and has even been dressed with artificial snow. The grounds feature magnolia, camphor, and palm trees, as well as two historic cannons.

A three-story frame hotel, "set among a profusion of tropic trees, shrubs and flowers," was built in downtown Santa Ana at Broadway and Sixth Street in 1921. St. Ann's Inn (named for Santa Ana's English equivalent) assumed the role of pampering 1920s visitors. Its advertisements offered "all the elegance, simplicity and home-like tone of old English inns, one-half hour over perfect roads to bathing beaches and golf links." Guests were assured of "every comfort and courtesy." The dining room for "special luncheons and dinners" made it a popular in-town stop. It also became a getaway resort for Hollywood stars who had slipped out of camera range to marry quietly in the picturesque nearby courthouse. During the Depression, inn clientele dwindled, and the county bought the hotel in 1931 to serve as an annex to the courthouse until 1969.

Orange County Civic Center Plaza is a grassy corridor with special meaning for many citizen groups. Along with monuments to war veterans, there is one honoring the county's firefighters—on Broadway next to the Hall of Administration, site of the historic St. Ann's Inn. Three white granite columns rising to a fire bell represent the past, present, and future of the fire service. Within the columns stands a fireman rescuing a child. The monument was designed and donated by the Orange County Fire Services Association in 1997. County fire departments also donated brass hose couplings and nozzles to be melted down and poured together to create the bell and statue. Black granite copies of their shoulder patches surround the base. Chosen to lend his likeness to the symbolic firefighter was the chaplain of both county and state fire personnel, Monsignor John Sammon, a vicar of the Diocese of Orange County.

Lumber was something boom-time Orange County needed but had to import. From the late 1880s onward, enormous quantities of boards sailed from Northern California and the Northwest to McFadden's Landing at Newport Beach. Cargoes were unloaded by a pony derrick onto open railcars of the McFadden Brothers' Santa Ana and Newport Railway, which carried them to the county seat. The brothers maintained this lumberyard at the end of the line in Santa Ana—the Newport Wharf and Lumber Company. There the boards were unloaded into inventory. The McFaddens eventually held interest in seventeen lumberyards. They also had redwood shingles shipped in that were then cured and dried by Santa Ana winds to reduce their weight for shipping east. The lumber company's 1895 downtown office (inset) was next door to the Orange County Title Company (later the First American Title Company), whose Orange County Archive was the major source of early photos in this book.

The short-line Santa Ana and Newport Railway would carry cargoes until 1933, but the site of this lumberyard continues to be a major shipping point for passengers. The land now holds the Santa Ana Regional Transportation Center between Sixth and Fruit streets. In the 1960s, the City of Santa Ana decided to replace the old Santa Fe Depot nearby. Then Amtrak took over all passenger rail operations, but they didn't build depots. So the city devised the concept of a regional transportation center that would serve not only train passengers but also bus and transit services. They decided to revive the mission-style depots that are so popular elsewhere to distinguish the city for incoming visitors. Meeting rooms on the fourth and fifth floors of the dramatic rotunda are decorated with historic transportation photos. The facility opened in 1985.

When Orange was laid out in 1871, the focal point was an open plaza square. The founders, two Los Angeles attorneys, named the cross streets for themselves: Chapman and Glassell. Later, a circular park was created within the square and traffic moved around it in a circle. This is a view looking toward East Chapman Avenue in the 1920s. Since agriculture was essential to the economy, pioneer residents planted grain and grapes, then tried walnuts and apricots. Eventually, Orange lived up to its name. By the time this photo was taken, that round citrus fruit had become the city's prime crop. Orange had the first citrus packing house in the county, from which the city's namesake was shipped all over the nation. Its first orange trees were two seedlings outside Captain Glassell's tract office on the plaza he helped design.

Today traffic circles around Orange Plaza in a one-way fashion, whereas before 1923 it had moved in both directions. In the early days, four of the eight corners around the plaza held a bank. The corners of East Chapman in the 1920s had the National Bank of Orange and the First National Bank of Orange, which later merged. At present, the same view toward East Chapman shows a Wells Fargo Bank on the site of the original Bank of Orange. On the right corner is the Carpenter Building—built in 1899 and remodeled in the

1980s. It is now Swift & Swift, accountants. The palm trees are gone and pines now hide the other buildings on the block. The star pine that has served as Orange's official Christmas tree through the years is less distinguishable. The plaza's original fountain stood there until 1937, then graced other locations, and was returned to the plaza (shown here) en route to a permanent home at the new library and history center.

In 1885, three years before Orange was incorporated, three hundred donated books housed in a downtown storefront were the nucleus for a city library. Then Orange, like many American cities, received a $10,000 grant from the Andrew Carnegie Foundation to build this library at Chapman Avenue and Center Street; it opened in 1908. The architectural design is documented as "Classical Revival, Type B" in the foundation's records. Other Orange County cities that received Carnegie library grants were Anaheim and Huntington Beach, Classic "Type C," and Santa Ana and Fullerton, "Mission/ Spanish Colonial." Each recipient of a grant had to provide a site and promise to support the library through local tax funds. In Orange, a small addition became necessary in 1930. In the 1950s, the city acquired a ten-acre parcel for a new civic center and library. However, a bond issue to fund the buildings failed, so the property was sold.

Thanks to the formation of a community support group, Friends of Orange Public Library, a bond issue was finally approved and the library pictured here opened on the old site in 1961. The city began acquiring property surrounding the old city hall across the street until it owned the entire block. In 1963, a $1.5 million, 54,000-square-foot civic center was built, but by the 1980s it was badly overcrowded. Some city departments were moved across the street to other city property. A new facility was built in 1990 for the Orange Police Department, opening up space for other city services. By the 1980s, the library itself needed expansion, but construction for an addition did not begin until 2005. The open frame of the addition is visible here on the far left, as the need for library services continues to grow with the population.

Whitewall tires and convertible roofs were the style of cars parked in 1922 on South Glassell Street in Orange, looking north from Almond Avenue. Diagonal parking was also in, along this block of one- and two-story buildings with individually intricate facades. The businesses included shoe stores on each side of the street. On the left were a real estate office, a drugstore, and the Colonial Theatre. On the right was Higgins Furniture Store, which opened in 1919, a family business of several generations. The palm trees in the distance mark the unique Orange Plaza Historic District, the city's spiritual heart, now listed on the National Register of Historic Places. Since 1973, it has been the site of an annual International Street Fair, which celebrates the community's rich heritage.

This photograph of South Glassell, with trees grown taller since the time it became an antiques mecca, has added an Army-Navy store among the shops featuring everything from American antiques to fine old furniture. The Higgins store, seen on the far right, tried to serve the trends of furniture over the years. In the 1950s it became Higgins Furniture and Antiques. The trend went from maple to chrome and Formica in the 1960s, Mediterranean in the 1970s, and traditional in the 1990s. Since the 1970s, Old Town Orange has become more and more a community of antique stores. Even the old Higgins building is now an antique mall.

More than a century ago, when the flatland of Orange County was robed in chaparral and cactus, a group of colonists from the Midwest, a Society of Friends, moved into what came to be called El Modena. In 1887, these Quakers hand-built a meetinghouse on a two-and-a-half-acre lot donated by four members of the congregation. David Hewes, a nearby citrus rancher and developer, gave them a large church bell, which they installed in the steeple. One month after the meetinghouse opened, a roaring Santa Ana wind pushed the new building from its foundation. The heavy bell crashed down and further damaged the building. So the Friends rebuilt their church, though they added better fortification against bad weather. Ninety years later, the congregation had outgrown that building, so they built again elsewhere, abandoning the old church.

By the 1920s, a large Mexican-American population had settled in El Modena, and today some newcomers assume the name is Spanish. Actually, it was named after the town of Modena in Italy. The "El" came later to satisfy the post office's concern that the name was too similar to Madera. The new residents needed stores and restaurants as well as places to live. In 1967, Javier and Nora Moreno discovered the empty old Friends Church building in El Modena and decided to convert it into Moreno's Mexican Restaurant on East Chapman Avenue. Its bright red roof and steeple are markers of its proud past. The outdoor dining patio is shaded by a giant California pepper tree, and strolling mariachis entertain the diners. Sections of El Modena were annexed to the City of Orange beginning in the 1950s.

Anaheim's first settlers in 1857 were German families who became successful in a new enterprise: growing grapes and making wine. A symbol of the wealth generated by the community was the impressive Metz Building. Here in the downtown Anaheim of 1889 sat a combination of architectural styles that sum up the sudden growth of that city. An Old West false-front building shares a block with the elegant Victorian Metz Building located at Center Street (now Lincoln Avenue) and South Los Angeles Street. That name would be changed to Anaheim Boulevard in the 1970s. Anaheim's second city hall is visible down the block at the far left. Gentlemen had gathered at Isaac Lyons' Hardware Store to inspect the sidewalk displays.

Orange County's first city is now its second most populous. Only Santa Ana, the county seat, exceeds it, and both cities boast more than 300,000 residents. Its civic complex consists of very modern buildings. In 1979, the ever-growing city moved its offices to City Hall East, seen on the left, and to this City Hall Annex building, which sits across the street from the old library. In 1992, city offices expanded again into the new eleven-story City Hall West, across the street from City Hall East. This city hall complex became the anchor for further central downtown development, including construction of a new public library. The old Carnegie library of 1908 is now the Anaheim Museum. Anaheim was Orange County's first incorporated city. Its charter mayor, Major Max Strobel, led the first move toward separation from Los Angeles County, which continued from 1869 until the creation of Orange County in 1889.

Walt Disney committed himself to designing a theme park that would entertain all ages and all members of a family. When the Santa Ana Freeway was constructed in the 1950s, Disney chose Anaheim as the hub of future population within eight Southern California counties. As Walt Disney dreamed of the Fantasyland he would bring to life in a 160-acre orange grove there, he saw the multitowered castle created by King Ludwig II high in the

German Alps. The authentic *schloss* was under construction from 1869 until 1886 and was never completed. Sleeping Beauty Castle took less than a year to build. It makes use of a movie set trick called forced perspective. Objects seem farther away than they really are. The first floor is full size, but higher up the scale is smaller. The castle's turrets only look full size, though the tallest rises only seventy-seven feet above the moat.

Fifty years later, Disney executives met to celebrate a half-century of entertaining children the world over. From its immediate success in Anaheim, the Disney organization has expanded operations to ten different theme parks, from Paris to Hong Kong, and has become the acknowledged theme-park pioneer. Now Disney theme parks attract a combined 100 million visitors annually, and with the Hong Kong park its latest investment, this figure is set to rise even further. The Matterhorn was added to Disneyland in 1959, and guests can still bobsled down it on two different tracks. These days, Space Station X-1 has been replaced by Buzz Lightyear's Astro Blasters; however, visitors are still able to enjoy the original 1955 ride, Snow White's Scary Adventures.

The premise of Disneyland's Tomorrowland was to predict the future. When the park opened in 1955 with its Rocket to the Moon attraction, the first actual landing on the Moon was still fourteen years away. Pictured here in the distance is the TWA-sponsored rocket, Moonliner, that introduced Disneyland visitors to the principles of the new science. Behind the scenes at Disney Studios, German rocket scientist Wernher von Braun had assisted in the early technical designs, both for the feature at Disneyland and the Disney television series. He would become director of the NASA flight center, and he masterminded the development of the rockets that would power the Gemini and Apollo missions.

Using updated space technology, Disney's Flight to the Moon replaced the Rocket in 1971. Then in 1975, that attraction advanced in time again to became Mission to Mars, continuing until 1992. Space Mountain first appeared in 1977 and was updated in 2005. Today, although the Magic Kingdom survives, Tomorrowland has been thoroughly overhauled. Other Orange County cities were already in the space race when Disney entered the field. Northrop Aviation in Anaheim was first in 1951, producing missiles and electronic systems. Ford Aerospace opened its Newport Beach operation in 1958 to design and make missile propulsion and guidance systems and went on to manufacture space and reentry vehicles. Rockwell International came to Anaheim in 1962 to produce missile guidance systems. North American Rockwell in Seal Beach manufactured the second stage of the Saturn V rocket that helped power the Apollo lunar landing in 1969.

Fullerton started life as a real Old West town. Growing up from the railroad tracks, it had its share of melodrama—construction camp scuffles and barroom brawls. The original Amerige Brothers' 1887 office, the first building in town, witnessed it all. The brothers convinced the Santa Fe Railway to change its course so it would run through the 430-acre town site they laid out. They got their way and named the place after the railroad agent, George Fullerton. Then the Ameriges aided residents needing help in real estate, insurance, or matters of the law. This undated scene outside their office appears to have a gold rush tie, with burros carrying returning prospectors. Many of the town's other buildings had a Western look, with signs painted on their false fronts. The blacksmith advertised "Artistic Horse Shoeing" and "Corns and Quarter Cracks Cured."

In 1904, Fullerton became Orange County's fourth incorporated city, after Anaheim, Santa Ana, and Orange. In 1917, the city opened its first public park on West Commonwealth Avenue, naming it for the enterprising founding brothers. This landmark building still stands in Amerige Park as the original real estate office that saw the start of this railroad town. Preserved with care, it hardly shows its age well over a century later. The park, which is on the site of the old Fullerton High School, played another historic role in the community.

Its baseball field once served as spring training grounds for teams in the old Pacific Coast League. The Hollywood Stars played there in the 1930s, the San Diego Padres and Sacramento Solons in the 1940s, and the original Los Angeles Angels in the 1950s. Joe DiMaggio came to bat there, and Orange County's own Walter Johnson dominated the pitcher's mound at what is now the home field of Fullerton's own young teams.

Farm wagons head south down Fullerton's Spadra (now Harbor Boulevard) in the 1890s. They carry a variety of local farm products to Fullerton's new (1888) Santa Fe station for shipping to market. Crossing Amerige and Commonwealth avenues on the way, they move past the two-story brick Fullerton Hotel, the neighboring pool hall, and a row of other distinctive buildings. Just a block away is where the Amerige brothers drove a stake into a wild mustard field in 1887 to mark their town site. Ahead is Santa Fe Avenue. Once the railroad came, the city was fast to develop, both as an agricultural center and as a shipping site. In fact, the *Fullerton News Tribune* reported that it was "the principal shipping point south of Los Angeles."

Today, at Harbor Boulevard and Amerige Avenue, stands Fullerton's landmark building, the Farmers and Merchants Bank. Though now it houses a collection of businesses and specialty shops, it was built in 1904 to be a bank. Fullerton's first bank played a significant role in the economics of the city. Its early officers were men like Charles Chapman and Samuel Kraemer, who had become wealthy from their citrus ranches and packing houses. After its initial forty years as a bank, the building became home to the Fullerton Music Company in 1944, enjoying that second life for another forty years. In 1989, the building was completely rehabilitated for its third life as Landmark Plaza, a commercial complex. What sets it apart is the elegant Beaux Arts facade it received in 1922. Its roof is crowned with a decorative parapet, and the exterior walls are embellished with tiled pilasters, recessed panels, molded trim, and floral motifs.

The railroad gave birth to Fullerton. And soon after it did, this impressive depot was built by the Santa Fe Railway. The frame Victorian station on Santa Fe Avenue, which opened for passenger and freight service in 1888, served the city until 1930. It was the last of the old-style stations in Orange County. A large, covered, pillared porch accommodated travelers waiting for trains in inclement weather. The depot underwent considerable expansion during its lifetime. Edward Amerige, cofounder of Fullerton, wrote about the impact of local rail services in 1904: "The town has since made remarkable strides in growth and advancement. Fullerton ranks today as one of the most important points in Southern California, being in about third place, in regard to number of [rail] cars of all kinds of products shipped annually in this part of the state and second to none in the County of Orange."

When this Spanish Revival–style depot replaced the old frame one in 1930, an editorial in the *Fullerton Daily News* pronounced: "Modern in keeping with the aspect of the city it serves, the new depot marks another milestone in the progress of the fastest growing city in Orange County. Its construction marks the recognition of Santa Fe officials of the size which Fullerton has attained." Even more remarkable is the fact that it is still in full service for train travelers seven decades later. When the Fullerton Redevelopment

Agency acquired ownership of this property in 1991, the depot was completely restored. This included removing the exterior paint to show the original varicolored stucco finish on the walls. It continues to serve as a full-service Amtrak passenger depot. In 1980, Fullerton's 1923 Union Pacific depot was moved onto the site with the Santa Fe's, also joining the 1917 Pacific Electric depot there, creating a major transportation center. The UP and PE depots are now restaurants.

By the 1870s, a number of people had settled along the Anaheim irrigation ditch in the Placentia area. They had helped dig the ditch and so became known as the Ditch People. They petitioned for a school, which opened in 1874—one room with twenty-six students on a two-acre site at Placentia and Chapman avenues. By 1898, two new rooms and a second story were added. A small, thirty-by-forty-foot lot within the school grounds was leased to Mrs.

Clara Wetzel for one dollar a month. There, in 1897, she built Placentia's first store, which contained its second post office. She was also allowed to have a dwelling there: her family poses in this photo. However, she had to waive all rights for damage from any schoolyard games. Before the end of the century, the school board granted permission to the Placentia Orange Growers Exchange to erect a packing house on one corner of the school grounds.

As oranges became the principal crop of Placentia, five more packing houses were built. This major industry thrived until the 1960s, when a disease called "quick decline" killed whole groves of trees. The packing houses began to close. However, the grove lands were able to support incoming population growth as residential communities were constructed there. The George Key

Ranch became a county historical park in 1980, preserving part of that pioneer grower's Placentia grove and home—a living monument to the citrus industry. Part of the early school site at Placentia and Chapman avenues now holds a McDonald's restaurant and PlayPlace.

Placentia was laid out as an actual town in 1910 and continued to add population until it outgrew its two-room school with 150 students. The school board called for a bond election to purchase a new site: eleven acres on Bradford Avenue. Though there was controversy about the expense, the bond issue passed. On Arbor Day of 1912, the pupils and teachers paraded from the old school to the new one under construction. Each class planted a small pepper tree there. This Bradford Elementary School building was an eyepopper, with two turret towers, an auditorium in the center, and classrooms at each end. An addition was completed around 1920. Though the school escaped damage in the 1933 Long Beach earthquake, during the fall of the very next year a raging fire rushed through it at night, destroying the building and its contents. A new eight-classroom school was soon erected.

The Placentia Citizens Committee appeared before the California Board of Education in 1933 with a petition asking for separation from the Fullerton High School District, where their students were in attendance. Granting of that request led to planning for Valencia High School, although in 1934 there was only one high school graduate. He presented a one-man play at the graduation ceremony, which had to be held in the Bradford Elementary School auditorium. Within months, that school burned down. A further shortage of classrooms caused by the fire meant that classes had to be held in churches. The first unit of Valencia High School was ready for classes in September 1935. Greatly expanded in segments since then, it is now under the jurisdiction of the Placentia–Yorba Linda Unified School District.

Two important things happened in Yorba Linda in 1913. The first, the original Fuerte avocado grove was planted; the second, Richard M. Nixon was born. Both of these events were destined to have a productive hold on the town into the future. Orange County's only native-born United States president was born and raised in this simple frame house on Yorba Linda Boulevard. It stands not far from the Pacific Electric Railway system's Yorba Linda station. Pacific Electric was a major force in Nixon's boyhood, since his father was a motorman on PE's Red Cars. The Nixon family home site, which had a private ten-acre lemon grove, was a neighbor to the city's two historic citrus packing houses.

Richard Nixon's home has been restored to its original 1910 condition. It now has the honor of being part of the nine-acre complex of the Richard M. Nixon Presidential Library, located at 18001 Yorba Linda Boulevard. Visitors can listen to an audio tour by Nixon himself, from a tape he made when the library was founded. He lived there for the first nine years of his life. The Nixon lemon grove became part of the grounds of the nearby

Richard M. Nixon Elementary School. His presidential library opened in 1990, funded as a private operation. In 2004, the U.S. Congress passed legislation making the Richard M. Nixon Presidential Library and Birthplace a federal operation. Locally, Imperial Highway (I-90) carries the name Richard M. Nixon Freeway.

OLINDA. OILFIELDS.

The first successful recovery of oil in Orange County was on its northern rim in the 1880s, first at Brea Canyon, then at Carbon Canyon, then south to the Coyote Hills. After one group of "wildcatters" tapped a significant oil-producing well in Carbon Canyon in 1896, they developed the Olinda camp, pictured here in 1910. The Santa Fe Railway had laid a track to the site to secure oil for its trains, creating the Santa Fe Camp. The northern hills of the county had come to be peppered with active petroleum rigs in the 1890s, with other oil camps building up around them. Then, as oil drilling ceased on the flat ground below the hills, the new town of Brea began to grow. By 1917 it was ready for incorporation, with a total of 732 inhabitants and 105 automobiles. When oil production dwindled in the 1940s, so did the population of Olinda, which eventually became a part of the city of Brea.

Instead of oil rigs penetrating the ground, there are now attractive residential communities. After the Carbon Canyon flood-control dam was built in the 1960s, land around it from the original Olinda town site became Carbon Canyon Regional Park. In addition to having all the characteristics of a county regional park, it has a ten-acre grove of about two hundred coastal redwood trees. Now Brea also has a museum within a city park that is devoted to the history of the oil industry there. It includes Olinda Oil Well No. 1, which was drilled in 1897. The Olinda Historic Museum and Park also includes the original field office and a jack line pump building. The park is run cooperatively by the City of Brea and the State of California.

A dozen years after it became a city, Brea designed and built its city hall. A successful bond issue authorized funding for a civic center, including a park and plunge (swimming pool). An entire block was purchased in the 1920s from Union Oil Company, and a Mission-style city hall with Art Deco ornamentation was designed. Opened in 1929, it was the first true civic center in Orange County. One building housed city offices and council chambers as well as courtrooms, a jail, a fire station, a library, and the chamber of commerce. Later, it would also house the Brea Historical Society's museum and offices.

By the 1970s, the need arose to expand the city center. A 500-acre parcel was set aside for both a new city hall and a cultural center. The old city hall was renovated and eventually became the Brea Scout Center in 2005, headquarters for all Boy and Girl Scout programs (Brea Boy Scouts originally began meeting in the 1920s in a log cabin). The restoration of the city hall building was undertaken by the Brea Lions Club to benefit many community groups. The unique building is listed on the National Register of Historic Places.

A "newcomer" to Orange County rail service, Union Pacific built a branch line from Whittier into Orange County (with stations at Anaheim, Fullerton, and La Habra), which was completed in 1923. This depot at La Habra was intended to handle mainly freight. It was located on Euclid Street, across from the sizable Pacific Electric depot, which had been in operation since 1909. Serving passengers as well as freight for farms and oil operations, the Pacific Electric was long a household name when Union Pacific arrived. Pacific Electric's Red Cars gave residents the convenience of traveling to the beach or to Los Angeles by simply stepping aboard. Union Pacific abandoned its tracks, donated this depot to the city of La Habra in 1956, and thereafter used the parallel Pacific Electric line. Valencia oranges from this city could fill up to two thousand railroad cars a season.

The City of La Habra leases this Mission-style train depot to the Children's Museum of La Habra. The 1923 Union Pacific depot has been fully restored and is listed on the National Register of Historic Places. Throughout the building there are interactive displays that children can touch and operate to expand their learning. The former depot waiting room is a nature walk exhibit, while the baggage room holds a working model-train layout. Other special features include a vintage carousel, a Kids on Stage mini-theater, a Science Station, and a Preschool Playpark. La Habra's 1909 Pacific Electric depot was moved across the street to be next door to the museum. It has been transformed into the Depot Playhouse, which includes children's productions in its seasonal schedule. A caboose outside the Children's Museum holds exhibits of local history, designed by the La Habra Old Settlers' Historical Society.

This is a view of La Habra Boulevard in 1917, one block from Euclid Street. The Glazier Brothers store, seen on the left, sold groceries, hardware, and general merchandise; their exterior walls and awnings served as signboards. The brothers built the first brick building in town, and Clarence Glazier was also postmaster. Delivery of mail quickened when it moved along the tracks of the Pacific Electric after 1908. Across the unpaved street on the right was the business of a "Practical Horseshoer." Traffic was a mix of horse-drawn vehicles and early motorcars. In those days, La Habra Boulevard was called Central Avenue. Euclid Street was Hiatt and was paved in 1915. It was reported that La Habra then had more paved streets than any other unincorporated town in California. It would become a city in 1925.

No old buildings remain in this view of La Habra Boulevard at Euclid. The Glazier store site is now part of Town Center, a complex of small businesses with driveways instead of wooden curbing, though the street is now well paved. The blacksmith shop site on the right has become part of a park and parking lot around the La Habra Civic Center. The palms seen in the distance identify the site of the La Habra Community/Senior Center. It stands where former President Richard Nixon had his first law offices. A plaque in that parking lot recalls that, when planning for the center began, Nixon indicated that he did not feel his offices had enough historical value to stand in the way of the civic project. Today La Habra Boulevard is temporarily shut down twice a year—for the Corn Festival and the I Love La Habra Fair.

After modest immigration by families in wagons, railroads brought new meaning to travel—as well as to shipping goods out and bringing businesses in. One of Orange County's first industrial firms came to Buena Park in 1889. The Pacific Condensed Milk, Coffee and Canning Company and its herd of cows settled in near the rails. The first evaporated milk cannery in California and Buena Park's first industry, it was known by its brand name, Lily

Creamery. Prior to the 1900s, unpasteurized milk held health risks. It quickly began to spoil after it left its origin. So milk was heated and canned to eliminate bacteria and extend its life. Buena Park became the county's first dairy center. Fresh milk still served the immediate populace, while condensed milk went by rail to Los Angeles and beyond. The creamery also held Buena Park's first library, from 1905 until 1907, when the factory closed.

Today the creamery site beside the railroad is also a site beside the Santa Ana Freeway at Beach Boulevard. It is now occupied by Ganahl Lumber Company, the oldest lumber firm in California. Founded in 1884 in Los Angeles, it came to Orange County first in Anaheim. The original products were lumber and cement. After the Anaheim yard opened in 1904, the firm took on a revolutionary product—plywood. Today Ganahl has several locations throughout Orange County. The Anaheim and Los Alamitos yards display rare old band saws retired from the Northwest lumber industry. They could cut logs up to ten feet in diameter and fifty-six feet long. The band saw has become Ganahl's logo. The Buena Park site carries an Orange County Historical Commission plaque, marking it as an early commercial site. The first lumber company at that location was the Buena Park Lumber Company.

Orange County even has an Old West ghost town. This 1950s photo is of "Main Street" in Buena Park, with a restaurant, miners' supply store, and jail. It started as a real berry farm in 1920 when Walter and Cordelia Knott leased twenty acres in Buena Park to raise berries. From a simple roadside stand, they sold varieties of their fresh berries, homemade pies, jams, and jellies. Walter turned the then-unknown hybrid boysenberry into a commercial success. The couple added a restaurant in 1934. Their home cooking became so popular that customers stood in line for it every day of the week. As a result, Walter pursued an idea to entertain them while they waited. During the 1940s and 1950s, he personally selected and imported Old West mining town buildings to create Knott's Ghost Town. It was a free-admittance tourist attraction with an authentic taste of educational entertainment.

This scene in the Ghost Town still looks the same after half a century, but it is only a part of what Knott's Berry Farm has become, and there is now an entry fee. Encompassing 150 acres, including the original farm site at Beach Boulevard and Knott Road in Buena Park, it calls itself "America's First Amusement Park." In addition to the original Ghost Town with added attractions, Knott's offers other themed areas: Indian Trails, Fiesta Village, the Boardwalk, Camp Snoopy, and Wild Water Wilderness. The Boardwalk began as a gypsy camp, then was transformed into a roaring twenties area. The park is now home to several major thrill rides, like the Perilous Plunge. Knott's Ghost Rider is the longest wooden roller coaster in the West; it begins in Ghost Town and travels through the park. The Supreme Scream sends riders down its 254-foot power tower in three seconds. Walter Knott's berry business has developed into a worldwide enterprise of signature jams and jellies.

As a young man, Edward Ware moved to the village of Garden Grove in 1876 and purchased forty acres. There he would build this stunning two-story Victorian home in 1891. Its high gables, and the extensive veranda that was added later, were common features of fine homes of this era. This photo was taken in about 1910. A pioneer in growing Valencia oranges, Ware surrounded his ranch house with a productive grove and led this special citrus to become the dominant product of his area. In fact, Ware became a noted horticulturist and was instrumental in developing soft-shelled Eureka walnuts. His daughter, Agnes Ware Stanley, gave two acres of the ranch to the Garden Grove Historical Society in 1970. Her son, Emerson, willed the society the Ware-Stanley House and its barn and tank house, which all became part of the Stanley Ranch Museum and Park.

The focal point of the Garden Grove Historical Society's museum village, the Stanley House features a fully furnished kitchen, the largest of its eight rooms. This was the all-purpose room—the site of cooking, churning, canning, tub bathing, and shaving, even before there was running water. Another highlight of the village is Walt Disney's original studio, a tiny frame garage now filled with Disney memorabilia and photographs. Other historic buildings on the site include Emerson Hall, which was Emerson Stanley's home and is now the historical society's offices; a general store; a barbershop; a blacksmith shop; a water tower; a windmill; an outhouse; and the town's first post office. Strawberry Lane is the private entrance to the village, named to honor the city's annual Strawberry Festival. There is a real strawberry patch as well. At various times during the past half century, Garden Grove has led the world in the production of chili peppers, poultry, and eggs, as well as strawberries.

Garden Grove's mix of red-tiled roofs and false-front facades was carried on into the 1940s. This is evident in this panoramic view of Euclid Avenue (now Historic Main Street) from Garden Grove Boulevard. Darling's (later Ogden's) drug store and Zlaket's Market are on the left. Schneider's open-front grocery store and Western Auto are on the right. Attempts had been made to incorporate as early as 1916, but cityhood would not come true for Garden Grove until 1956, when it was endorsed by both the Improvement Association and the Businessmen's Association. The building boom of the 1920s almost doubled the town's population, as did post–World War II arrivals, so an organized government became the only way to properly serve the needs of the people.

In the 1970s, the entire street and curbs on this block of Euclid Avenue were taken up from one side to the other in a major capital improvement. It prompted the name change to Historic Main Street, the original heart of the city. Zlaket's Market, founded in 1927, is the only original store remaining on the block. London plain trees line the entire length of this street, once only a village path. The early town's first Grover's Day celebration in 1939 was held in Euclid Park, enhanced by a WPA-built bandstand. Grover's Day later became the annual Strawberry Festival. By the time Garden Grove was celebrating its twentieth anniversary, its park inventory had grown from this one to eighteen. The second park was surplus property from World War II: Army Air Force Haster Field. The city also has a park dedicated to children: Atlantis Play Center. This sea-themed playground includes a creative Viking ship, flying sea horses, dolphins to ride, and a slide named Danny Sea Dragon.

While Anaheim was founded as a grape-growing and wine-making colony, Westminster's start was dedicated to the opposite lifestyle—religious temperance. It was a farming community where wine grapes were not allowed to be grown. Presbyterian minister Lemuel Webber bought a tract of 6,500 acres in 1870. The town that rose there was named for his admiration of the Westminster Assembly of 1642, which prescribed the concepts of the Presbyterian faith. He welcomed residents who shared his ideals of religion and morals. The first church was built in 1879 and burned down in 1915. This is the replacement, built at the same location on Westminster Boulevard. Two new features were an artistic stained-glass window and a windmill-assisted well. The residents worked to overcome the swampy nature of the local soil, turning thousands of acres into one of the most productive celery fields in the world. Twelve thousand bunches an acre were harvested in a peak year.

For nearly a decade, Westminster citizens abided by the code of "no manufacturing, buying or selling intoxicating beverages except for sanitary or scientific purposes." A saloon broke the spell in 1880 but soon closed. Grapes for raisins were grown successfully. The congregation was then able to purchase ten acres of land. There a new church, a fellowship hall, and educational buildings were completed near the original site on Westminster Boulevard. When the town became a city in 1957, it took on an English theme because of its Westminster legacy. The civic center has a small clock tower mimicking the look of London's Big Ben, and many buildings are "half-timbered," Old English style. Street signs are written in Old English script. The 1980s found Vietnamese refugees settling into Orange County, establishing businesses and homes. Thanks to them, today Westminster and Garden Grove have the distinction of a unique ethnic attraction with freeway signs directing tourists to Little Saigon.

Tom Talbert and his family take off for a motor jaunt from his downtown office in Huntington Beach in this 1906 photo. In the late 1890s, many families moved into the county, having heard about the rich farmland waiting within the wide bend of the Santa Ana River. There were ample natural springs throughout the area, making irrigation easy. In truth, there was too much water for most farm crops, enhanced by frequent river flooding. In

1903, the Talbert Drainage District was formed by the Talbert brothers to control the path of the water. Talbert also became the name of the developing town, where Tom Talbert's general store held the post office. He also busied himself with selling real estate. Wild celery flourished in the peat bogs, so celery was one of the crops tested to grow commercially. When it succeeded, Tom Talbert was ready to sell celery farm acreage.

Success in real estate led Tom Talbert into politics. He served for more than twenty years as a member of the Orange County Board of Supervisors. His voting address was in Huntington Beach, but he is not forgotten in the neighboring town named for him. His original real estate branch office in Talbert is preserved within a picket fence in Heritage Park near Talbert Avenue. Its wall signs indicate that he had advanced from celery farms to oil investments, another major commodity of that area. A Talbert Incorporation Committee was formed in 1956, and the city of Fountain Valley was established the following year. This name honored the artesian wells that had led to its settlement by farmers. It had also been jokingly called Gospel Swamp. The charter city council members were all farmers, and among themselves they elected Jim Kanno as the first Japanese-American mayor in the mainland United States.

Los Alamitos began as a vast company beet farm. Its centerpiece from 1897 until 1926 was the huge factory that processed the beets into sugar. Here, across the tracks on Main Street, the Los Alamitos Sugar Company stands boldly across the end of Sausalito Street. The company town around the factory, which employed four hundred, included worker housing and a clubhouse. There were two hotels, a pool hall, bars, and other treats for bachelor workers. In 1911 alone, the factory processed 180 million pounds of beets. This photo was taken around that time; it shows a town that looks like it belongs on the old frontier. Real shootings and stabbings, along with false-front businesses, brought Hollywood. It was a ready-made setting for Western movies. But by 1926, the factory closed because a worm had destroyed the beet crop. In 1932, Dr. Ross Company leased it to make dog and cat food. The 1933 earthquake severely damaged the brick structure, but the factory continued to make pet food until 1943.

From the time Los Alamitos was laid out around the first sugar-beet factory in Orange County until it closed in 1926, a rail line served it and the residents. Now they depend Interstate 605, the San Gabriel Freeway, for transportation. Curbs, paving, and stop signs are now part of Reagan Street, the present name of Main Street (it was renamed for the owner of an early water agency). The flag reveals a major tenant (the U.S. Postal Service), which came to town in 1995, here hidden behind a grand palm tree. Los Alamitos incorporated in 1960. Until then, the chamber of commerce acted as town organizer, acquiring traffic signals and street lighting—even seeing that a sewer district was created and a school bond was passed. The sugar factory was finally razed in 1960. Now a smaller business building marks the end of Reagan Street. Los Alamitos is still a border town—on the border between Orange County and Los Angeles County at Coyote Creek.

This general store in Los Alamitos was typical of those in outlying areas. Their specialty in the 1910s was their comprehensive all-in-one service. Felts Co., "the home of Los Angeles Grocery Co.," carried meat and groceries, gasoline, tires, and hardware. It even served as the Los Alamitos post office, complete with its identifying American flag and a bird sitting on the flagpole. An early pickup truck (far right) stands ready to deliver. And there was usually someone standing around waiting to be of service. Before there was a sugar beet farm or town, there was Rancho Los Alamitos. It was granted in 1784 to Manuel Nieto when he retired from the California army of the Spanish king. Rancho land was purchased in 1881 by John Bixby and I. W. Hellman. William Clark, a future U.S. senator, bought 8,000 acres from them in 1896 to build the factory, then created the Los Alamitos town site around it.

This post office has served the Los Alamitos community since 1995. The postal service there has as colorful a history as the city itself. The first post office opened at Catalina and Pine, across the street from the railroad station, in 1897, as the sugar beet factory was opening. By 1907, the post office had relocated to Felts Market and General Store. It was next located in the home of the postmaster, who was also president of the chamber of commerce. After his retirement, the post office moved to a storefront on Los Alamitos Boulevard, and many businesses followed. During the first few years following World War II, the city's population soared. So in 1962, a larger building was allotted for mail services. By the 1990s, the city's population had earned the present building, which is situated very near the grounds of the sugar beet factory that had started the town.

In 1947, unincorporated Los Alamitos got a new county fire station on South Los Alamitos Boulevard. It was manned by a devoted group of volunteers. The double-bay station had a hose-drying tower in the rear yard. After each fire call, the cotton hose was hung to dry to prevent mildew, a standard practice at the time. What was unusual is that between 1947 and 1953, Orange County constructed ten nearly identical volunteer fire stations made of adobe brick, the earthy building material of early mission days. State forestry labor assisted in the construction. To further their tie to the local past, these stations were adorned with Spanish red-tile roofs. The adobe brick maker who supervised the project had also supplied Walter Knott with adobe bricks for the Ghost Town and Steak House at Knott's Berry Farm. Knott donated land for the fire station built at his park. It still stands and is now used as the park's accounting office.

Now only two of the original ten adobe buildings are still in use as fire stations: at Sunset Beach and Trabuco. This restored Los Alamitos station, first of the adobes to be built, is now a museum, created and maintained by the Los Alamitos Museum Association. In addition to a pictorial history of the local past, the museum holds a hall of fame that honors residents who have earned national or international recognition in their fields. Museum artifacts include vintage medical equipment, household goods, books, and an antique fire cart. The vintage hose-drying tower outside has been transformed into a clock tower. Of the other remaining adobe stations, Huntington Beach's is a liquor store, Garden Grove's is VFW Post 6475, and the one in Cypress stands empty. The Tustin site is now a diner. The Silverado adobe station was destroyed by a mudslide during torrential rains in 1969. Ironically, the metal-clad building that replaced it was heavily damaged in a 1989 fire.

During the height of wine production in the 1860s and 1870s, the German colony in Anaheim created Orange County's first port, naming it Anaheim Landing. Wagon trains carried wine, wool, and grain twelve miles to the coast, where goods were shuttled by lighters (barges) to sailing ships bringing in lumber and supplies. Each summer, entire families would join the wagons heading to the coast to escape the inland heat. They pitched tents or built temporary shacks near the short pier and warehouse, enjoying a vacation at the seashore, as this circa-1890 photo shows. Eventually some small houses were built, as some visitors became full-time residents. Anaheim Landing would become part of Seal Beach. As the Pacific Electric Railway made its way down the coast, it took over shipping goods to larger ports. A larger pier was built in 1906, and the warehouse, by then little used, was converted to a bathhouse.

In this picture, taken from the edge of Anaheim Bay, Catalina Island is silhouetted as a cargo freighter passes by in one of the nation's busiest sea corridors. Since World War II, Anaheim Landing has been absorbed into the Naval Weapons and Ammunition Depot, which loads and services large military ships, including destroyers and cruisers. To accommodate them, the old wine port was dredged to a forty-foot depth. In 1962, with guided missiles added to its stock, the base was renamed Seal Beach Naval Weapons Station. The government also purchased the land that was the Seal Beach Airport, a base for gliders and small aircraft. Nearly 1,000 of the Navy's 5,000 acres have comprised a National Wildlife Refuge since 1972, protecting the habitat of indigenous birds and fish. Migrating birds from as far away as South America and Alaska also use the refuge as a rest stop.

The Joy Zone amusement park's eighty-by-ninety-foot pool (in the pavilion) and the wooden roller coaster beyond, then called the Derby, had a difficult time competing with the beach itself in the 1920s. Visitors landing there could arrive with a picnic lunch or purchase one from one of the pushcart vendors that roamed through the scene. Babies played safely in the sand, while others waded into the water. There were wicker-covered electric cars to rent. For those who stayed the evening, fifty large scintillator lights installed at the end of the pier, left over from the Panama Pacific Exposition, cast rainbow colors in the water. Weekends brought fireworks. This pavilion housed not only the pool but an arcade of shops and games alongside it. The popular candy sold there was produced by an on-site factory. The Joy Zone was the place to be through the 1920s, until the Depression of the 1930s lessened leisure cash for the working class. The roller coaster burned down in the late 1920s.

The Seal Beach pier is still there, though now it holds a restaurant at the seaward end and a fishing supply shop. A bronze sea lion patrols the pier's entry, reminding visitors that it was sea lions, not seals, that once dominated the beach. The mile-long beach is still there, though it no longer holds enclosed entertainment facilities in pavilions. However, youngsters have their own "Joy Zone" on the sand, with climbing and swinging rides enclosed by a safety fence. Condominium and apartment dwellers enjoy a wide ocean view. City-installed sand berms at the edge of the beach will hopefully control the potential intrusion of high tides. Main Street Seal Beach reflects the atmosphere that identifies this city as a small beach town.

The Holly Sugar Company, which had been in the business for more than a decade, felt that electric power would be the coming thing in the industry. The first all-electric sugar-beet processing factory was built in Huntington Beach in 1911, near Main Street between Garfield and Yorktown. This photo was taken circa 1920. The factory spurred growth in the beach community for several years—until oil was discovered on the property. At one time, about seventy square miles of Orange County were planted with sugar beets. Electricity even carried away the processed sugar from this plant, via Pacific Electric Railway's freight trains. Factory workers and residents also traveled on the Red Cars of Pacific Electric. By the 1920s, as the sugar-beet industry was waning, this plant was converted for use as an oil refinery.

Today the general area of Huntington Beach around the huge sugar-beet factory site holds a variety of smaller businesses along Main Street, a bit inland from the coast. This one is also "powered by electricity," specializing in the far-reaching electronic advertising field. In contrast to a company that produced a tangible product like sugar, Ocean Media, Inc., produces intangible direct-response advertising for e-commerce companies. Founded in 1996 in Huntington Beach, it has moved into national media circles with its specialty clientele: dot-com companies. These have included Priceline.com, Overstock.com, BestBuy.com, Register.com, and FreeCreditReport.com. While it is nationally known for handling e-commerce, it also does the media planning and buying of other forms of advertising—broadcast and cable television, radio, print, and outdoor media.

Life changed in Huntington Beach when oil was first discovered there in 1920. This photo, shot in the 1920s from the municipal pier, shows how wooden oil rigs took over the coast, leaving only enough room for an indoor saltwater pool, the building on the right. It didn't, however, affect enjoyment of the beach itself. The first oil strike was modest, but the second was a serious gusher that produced two thousand barrels of oil a day. Suddenly there was the need for

housing for oil workers, so every structure in sight was converted to living quarters—even barns and garages. In the process of recovering this natural resource, as many as three hundred homes that had enjoyed an ocean view were moved inland out of the way of the oil operations. Oil strikes in various sections of town came over a period of decades. By the 1970s, the highly flammable wood derricks had been removed and were replaced by metal rigs.

Nature provided Huntington Beach with miles of wide, sandy beaches that are used to perfection by waders and surfers of all ages. Here, a group of stark white condominiums has replaced the saltwater plunge, and palm trees have replaced the oil derricks. The winter beach draws fewer swimmers, though some bold surfers insulate themselves with wet suits against the colder ocean water. Shorebirds migrate along this coast; some are visible at the far right of the beach. Red-tiled roofs of newer downtown developments are visible through the trees on the right. Oil is still procured, though it is now done through slant drilling, eliminating the need for rigs directly over the oil deposit.

In 1910, the date of this photo, heavily clad beachgoers at Huntington Beach had the added entertainment of a concert from an acoustic municipal band shell. Those who chose to walk the entire length of the pier had a thousand-foot stroll. Huntington Beach's first pier was built of wood in 1904. The bandstand was located next to the pier, at about Fifth Street. The original name given to Huntington Beach in 1901 by Philip Stanton and his partners was Pacific City. He hoped it would rival Atlantic City in New Jersey. Eighteen months later, Stanton sold his 1,500 acres to a syndicate that included Henry Huntington, hence the name change. Besides building the first pier, the syndicate brought Huntington's Pacific Electric Railway through town.

With both a state and a city beach, Huntington Beach boasts more than eight miles of nearly continuous wide strand. The reliable surf there is famous, making it the natural venue for international surfing contests. In fact, Huntington Beach calls itself Surf City, U.S.A. There is a Surfing Walk of Fame and an International Surfing Museum that displays the evolution of surfboards from the huge heavy wooden ones of early days to the current sleek, foam-and-acrylic-resin models. Rebuilt several times over the years, this municipal pier is now more than 1,800 feet long. Ruby's Diner has added a note of ruby color at the end of the pier, which is floodlit at night. Huntington Beach entertains as many as 9 million visitors a year.

This early 1930s scene, taken from the Huntington Beach pier looking south, shows a cross-section of the city's leisure life. While the sea accommodates swimmers and waders, the beach offers sandy seats under umbrellas, and it supports picnic tables, benches, tents, and playgrounds. A Standard Oil Company tank car on the train track recalls the presence of the oil industry. Off the left side is the Pacific Electric station. On the street behind the tracks at left is the famous 1929 Golden Bear restaurant and music hall. To its right is the multiarched Macklin Building, once an automobile sales agency. It is rumored that its underground garage became a speakeasy connected to the Golden Bear during Prohibition days. A lone oil rig towers over the power lines of the residential area at the right.

Even in Southern California, this off-season beach scene is only a whisper of the way it appears on a busy summer weekend. A lone gabled house remains of the earlier group of large homes. Most of the buildings in the Main Street pier area, built early in the twentieth century, are gone, as redevelopment has changed the scene. One new project is Plaza Almeria, a Spanish-style complex offering retail businesses and offices, town houses, and penthouses.

The oldest building in Costa Mesa dates from the early 1800s and has lasted through the changes of contrasting lifestyles since then. The Diego Sepulveda Adobe is believed to have been built as an outpost of Mission San Juan Capistrano. It sheltered herdsmen who tended cattle grazing freely throughout the area and welcomed padres and visitors traveling from Mission San Juan Capistrano to Mission San Gabriel. In Spanish it was called an *estancia*, or way station. During Mexican rule, it became the headquarters for Diego Sepulveda on his section of Rancho Santiago de Santa Ana. Later, it was the home of Gabe Allen, a veteran of the Civil War who retired to California. The adobe was donated to the city of Costa Mesa in 1963 by the Segerstrom family, much of whose original farmland holdings are today within that city.

The Costa Mesa Historical Society has created a museum within the historic Sepulveda Adobe. Details of the various types and sizes of its adobe bricks are visible within the interior walls. Rooms of the adobe have been furnished with pieces from the various eras through which the structure has been inhabited. It became a private home during the rancho period from the 1820s to the 1840s. Showcases display artifacts of Spanish and Mexican origin. The estancia site is at the top of a knoll within a ten-acre city park at Adams Avenue and Mesa Verde Drive. Public tours are given by the historical society, which also maintains a museum within another city-owned building. That one includes a city history and a military collection harkening back to World War II, when part of Costa Mesa was the Santa Ana Army Air Base.

During the first half of the 1900s, much of southern Orange County was the most productive bean field in the world, covering thousands of acres and looking like this early photo at harvesttime. Beans proved to be the most successful local crop for dry farming: cultivation without irrigation. Lima beans and black-eyed peas were especially popular for their high protein content. The Segerstrom family had migrated from Sweden in 1898 to farm. They leased twenty acres in Costa Mesa and pioneered the production of lima beans there. By the 1950s, they owned many times that acreage, planted primarily with beans. Third-generation landowner, Henry Segerstrom, turned those fields into a harvest to "feed" locals and visitors by satisfying their shopping appetites. In 1967, he plowed under some of the bean fields to create the world-class South Coast Plaza, which has become one of the largest retail centers in America. Then he devised a plan to satisfy Orange County cultural appetites.

The now internationally renowned Orange County Performing Arts Center opened in 1986 in the center of another Segerstrom bean field in Costa Mesa. The acreage needed for this 3,000-seat showplace was donated by the family. Symphony and opera companies, dancers, and musicians from around the world bring to Orange County the culture of many countries in this elegant venue. Dramatic in design, the center itself was paid for by private donations.

Two new concert halls are being added on additional donated acreage. Just a block away is a secluded sculpture garden called California Scenario, designed by noted sculptor Isamu Noguchi. Among art pieces representing such themes as a desert garden, there is a sculpture made of fifteen giant granite "beans," forming the twenty-eight-ton "Spirit of the Lima Bean," symbolizing its significance in the development of Orange County.

NEWPORT BEACH, STATION AND WHARFF, CAL.

A crowd of Orange County inlanders pose during a 1901 outing in Newport Beach. Their train waits at the depot to return them to Santa Ana. In 1888, the McFadden brothers, who had used a landing inside Newport Bay as their shipping port, expanded their business seaward by constructing McFadden's Wharf, which extended 1,200 feet into the ocean. Railroad tracks were laid along it, then continued for eleven miles inland. This Santa Ana and Newport Railway was ready in 1891 to shuttle goods and people between the two cities, connecting with the Santa Fe in Santa Ana. The short-line railroad carried as much as 70,000 tons of freight and 12,000 passengers a year. Here, cranes and railcars show that the wharf was meant for commercial traffic, not passengers. On the beach, beside the wharf pilings, are early dory boats that took fishermen out to sea each morning.

Today's Newport Pier, though rebuilt several times, occupies the same location as the original wharf built in 1888. This landmark is the popular focus of everyday beach and water activities and special events. Feet, bare or not, tread its length every day, whether they arrived by foot, bike, or some other vehicle. The train tracks are gone, while the city lifeguard headquarters has replaced the depot. A tackle shop thrives at the end of the pier. Fishermen, not boaters, rule this corner of the Newport scene. The sandy beach extends for six miles, broken only by another wooden pier at Balboa. The dory fishermen, as in the early days, continue to make their morning run, returning to this beach to sell their fresh catch.

This mid-1920s photograph of Newport Bay reveals the many facets of ocean life already developing during that era. Taken from the Balboa Peninsula looking southeast across the bay to Balboa Island's beachfront cottages, the farther view shows the coastline at Corona del Mar. In addition to the mainland and this peninsula, Newport Beach consists of several man-made islands. Balboa Island is the largest and most populous and public. On Balboa Peninsula itself, the star landmark was the 1905 Balboa Pavilion, at far right.

Beside it a shed protects small boats, while other trappings of boating are visible. Sailboats moving through the bay foreshadow the small-craft harbor that would be created here. Balboa Peninsula, separating the harbor from the ocean, is a natural sandpit that resulted from longtime silting of the Santa Ana River before its course was controlled to construct Newport Harbor, which opened in 1936.

Now nearly obscuring the historic pavilion, boats of all sizes cluster along the Balboa Peninsula. A popular attraction on the boardwalk here is the Fun Zone, a miniature amusement park enjoyed by each generation since it opened in 1936. Its iconic Ferris wheel and carousel have weathered the decades, joined more recently by kiddie rides, bumper cars, and an arcade. An average of one thousand passengers a day are shuttled between Balboa Island and Balboa Peninsula by the ferry, which has been in operation since 1909. The Fun Zone Boat Co. offers harbor sightseeing cruises aboard the *Tiki*, seen here at left, as well as on the smaller *Queen* and *Belle*. A fleet of Jet Ski rentals lines the dock. The Fun Zone was given historic status by the California Coastal Commission in 1975 and then underwent a complete renovation in the 1980s.

When the Pacific Electric rail line was headed south from Long Beach, Orange County's coastal towns got in line to woo a stop within their developing communities. Newport and Balboa promoters designed their idea as a waterfront "depot" on the peninsula—naming it Balboa Pavilion, a Victorian boat- and bathhouse. It was completed in 1905 and was photographed here just before the first Pacific Electric Red Car arrived that year. The Hotel Balboa beside it was built in only ten days to accommodate all the expected visitors. In 1906, Newport Beach became a city; Balboa Island was annexed a decade later. The Balboa Ferry came into being in 1909 to shuttle visitors between Balboa Island and the peninsula. The ferry started as a rowboat, then was built to carry one car, and now carries passengers and three cars. The pavilion, created as a symbol of the city's promising tourism future, has itself become the focal point for tourist activities.

It was a big-band ballroom in the 1930s, a ten-lane bowling alley in the 1950s, and has held both a post office and a seashell museum. Then the Balboa Pavilion was restored in the 1960s to extend its life even further. This brought it to be named a California State Historical Landmark; it also earned a listing on the National Register of Historic Places. Today it is the terminal for sportfishing and cruise boats around the harbor and to Catalina Island.

It hosts the Harborside Restaurant and Grand Ballroom. Surrounding the pavilion is one of the largest small-craft harbors in the United States, berthing 10,000 private boats and yachts. Multimillion-dollar homes of celebrities and executives surround the boating channels. By night, the pavilion's roofline and cupola are illuminated, extending its duties even further as it becomes a "lighthouse."

The Balboa Peninsula's long sandy beach was dotted first with visitors' tents, then small one-story cottages in the early years of the twentieth century, when this photo was taken. The view south along Balboa Beach shows how many cottages began to line the shore. They were first seasonal rentals, but they progressed to being full-time homes as the transportation network around Newport Bay improved. Most swimmers would actually "surf bathe," hampered from moving out too far from shore by the weight of their full-body wool bathing suits.

Balboa Beach has been named one of the top ten urban beaches in the United States by *Surfrider* magazine. This view was taken from the Balboa Pier, Newport's second pleasure pier. The beach at Balboa is much wider now, since the bay was dredged in the 1930s to create harbor channels. The residue was deposited along the shore. The cottages are small only in comparison to the large estates and gated community homes that are prevalent in other parts of Newport Beach. From here the beach heads farther south into a jetty, forming the notorious Wedge, where waves can reach fantastic heights in shallow water—and where local surfing legends are born.

The newly paved Coast Highway of the late 1920s crossed Newport Bay on a wooden trestle bridge near the Bay Shore Camp. All-day parking or overnight tent camping cost twenty-five cents at this location. Fast food and bait were sold at the stand by the road, along with gas from the round glass pump. Newport's Upper (or Back) Bay is visible in the background. This bridge carried the first traffic along the new Pacific Coast Highway in 1927, curving around the cliffs of Castaways Point, seen at left. This site, near Dover Drive, is close to the original Newport Landing of the 1870s, where ships first ventured into Newport Bay and anchored, thus originating the name "New Port." Beginning in 1889, vessels used the facilities at the oceanfront McFadden's Wharf instead.

The sleek, seven-lane Pacific Coast Highway concrete bridge has crossed Newport Bay since 1981. From it, some motorists are surprised to see the paddle-wheel steamboat that lies anchored at the shore. Once the Reuben E. Lee restaurant, it has for years been the Newport Harbor Nautical Museum, containing historical exhibits of the area, rotating nautical exhibits, and a world-class model-ship collection. What was the Bay Shore Camp in the 1920s is now the exclusive Bay Shore community of luxury homes fronting on the harbor. Its most famous resident was actor John Wayne, who moored his yacht *Wild Goose* there. Castaways Point, off the left of this photo, now holds a natural park developed by the City of Newport Beach. Its seventeen acres have trails leading through the natural habitat, and a demonstration garden is planted with the native California plants that support it.

In the mid-1950s, some seventy North American bison were imported to take up residency at the Buffalo Ranch on MacArthur Boulevard, a mile inland from the Pacific Coast Highway. The ranch was actually an entertainment venue on land leased by the Irvine Company to "rancher" Gene Clark. A winding road through their grazing grounds enabled visitors to drive through and see the grand creatures up close. The shaggy beasts, symbols of the Old West, had been trucked in from Kansas. The herd included a couple of Brahmalos—a crossbreed between Brahma cattle and bison (the preferred name for buffalo). In keeping with popular history, there was an Indian village of teepees (more typical of Kansas than California) with Native American "residents" also originally rooted elsewhere. The look was completed with an Indian trading post and themed rides.

By the 1960s, as upscale housing developments crept closer to the buffalo and Fashion Island was being developed nearby, both the herd and the ranch were reduced in size. The Indians and the trading post were first to go. When there were only a few animals remaining, the whole operation packed up and left. However, realizing the unique tenant it had hosted, the Irvine Company set aside a small grassy oasis and commissioned a larger-than-life-size bronze bison to honor the Buffalo Ranch and its unique residents. The Bison Monument stands at MacArthur Boulevard and Bonita Canyon Road, in memory of the most unusual animal species to graze on the Irvine Ranch. A plaque at the base of the statue tells the story. The largest real-life bull there weighed more than a ton—even more than his bronze counterpart. The sculptor was noted wildlife specialist Martha Pettigrew, whose museum-piece subjects include thoroughbred horses.

Based on archaeological digs, people have lived in Crystal Cove for thousands of years. Then came beachcombers, squatters, and artists. They built driftwood shelters with palm-thatched roofs in the 1920s. This was part of the Irvine Ranch, between Newport Beach and Laguna Beach. Its owner tolerated respectful individuals slipping in and building what pleased them, as long as everybody else liked it. It was one part of James Irvine II's domain that developed with no interference. Beginning in the 1930s, renters reinforced their cottages—more than forty—and the area continued to look haphazard. Somehow this cove succeeded in bridging the gap between Newport society and Laguna casual. Hollywood loved this setting that was caught in a time warp. Even as luxury ocean-view properties developed around it with sky-high prices, Crystal Cove remained untouched.

When the State of California agreed to preserve this 3.2-mile coast in the 1970s, Crystal Cove State Park was created. Now there are designated hiking trails and camping sites around the cove of ramshackle cottages. However, the decision was to preserve the cottages, too, capturing a lifestyle elsewhere changed. Maybe Laguna's Plein Air painters saved it. When their paintings of Crystal Cove decorated with human flotsam were hung in museums, how could anyone destroy the subject? So the state moved the renters out and is refurbishing cottages as they were, preparing to rent them to others who want to share this lifestyle, even if only for a short time. The movie *Beaches*, starring Bette Midler, was filmed here.

Laguna Beach is justly known as a city of art and artists, and of festivals and pageantry celebrating them. The scenic coast of southern Orange County—cliffs overlooking coves and beaches with a backdrop of mountains—has attracted artists to paint and settle here since the late 1800s. During the Depression, hungry artists hung their paintings along the road to attract buyers. This evolved into the annual Festival of Arts. In 1933, the staging of what would become the world-famous Pageant of the Masters came into being: *tableaux vivants*—famous works of art staged with living models. Impressed with what this art colony was doing, the Irvine Company gave the city six acres for an art venue in 1941. This, the Irvine Bowl and its grounds, became the permanent home of the festival and the pageant.

The Pageant of the Masters has made the Irvine Bowl in Laguna Beach a world-class venue. Funded by the Festival of Arts Association, the basic outdoor amphitheater opened in 1941, with promise of a permanent stage, seating, lighting, and sound equipment as funds became available. World War II kept it from a second season until 1946. Since then, the summer seasons have been continuous. There are 2,600 audience seats and an orchestra pit out front. When actress Bette Davis was a resident of Laguna Beach in the 1940s, she appeared one summer in Joshua Reynolds's painting of actress Sarah Siddons, *The Tragic Muse*. Davis also helped paint numbers on the bowl seats. Actress Teri Hatcher and her daughter were volunteer posers recently.

Where but in Laguna Beach is there a Main Beach instead of a Main Street? The community that grew up around the beach saw activity there progress beyond sand and water fun. The boardwalk in this 1920s photo led to the Cabrillo Ballroom. South of it was the combination of local hotels, moved together to form the original Laguna Hotel, which held the town's first art exhibit. However, by the 1950s, this beach had evolved into a series of dens and dives, including the notorious Dante's Inferno. At that point, a beautification council began the drive to restore the city's "Window on the Sea." By 1968, the receptive city had purchased one thousand feet of Main Beach oceanfront, and the offending buildings were razed.

Main Beach in today's Laguna Beach provides an open, noncommercial view of surf and sand—enjoyable even from the traffic lanes. It is popular with swimmers, surfers, scuba divers, fishermen, walkers, joggers, and plain and simple beach lovers. Hotel Laguna, the prominent coastal landmark seen in the center, has been a hotel site since 1886. The original hotel complex gave way in 1930 to this towered treasure, remodeled over the decades. Several spots along the coast have lookout points, such as the palm-treed overlook at Heisler Park. In addition to the beachfront, Laguna is bordered by about 17,000 acres of greenbelt, which includes the only natural lakes in Orange County.

TREASURE ISLAND

It's really not an island and has no pirate's treasure, but the name of this point of land in southern Laguna Beach known as Treasure Island developed its own rules. By the 1950s, as pictured here, it had become a popular trailer park off Pacific Coast Highway. In the 1880s, the Goff brothers built a hotel there. But there was no coastal road yet, and there were few tourists to house. Eventually, what was first called Goff Island passed into other hands. Movies shot there in the 1920s included *Evangeline*, in which it was portrayed as the Nova Scotia coastline. Then, in the 1930s, some scenes of the famous MGM movie, *Treasure Island* starring Wallace Berry, were filmed here. From that celebrated moment, the area took on the movie's name. After that, it became an exclusive residential trailer park with a private beach and pier. Hollywood was back in 1954 to film scenes for the Lucille Ball–Desi Arnaz hit comedy, *The Long, Long Trailer*.

During the 1990s, concerns were raised when plans were made for a multimillion-dollar resort and private community to replace the Treasure Island trailer park. In modified form, with community input, the concept for the new Montage Resort was finally approved. It opened in 2003. Laguna Beach's fame as an art colony with modest beginnings tinted the design of this 262-room resort on thirty seaside acres. It carries through an early-1900s look with beach bungalow–style rooms, each with a balcony and ocean view. The entire complex features a collection of fine art inspired by the early California Arts and Crafts movement, of which Laguna was a part. Wisely, the new-generation planners preserved two palm trees lovingly named for Lucille Ball and Desi Arnaz, planted when one of their scenes was being filmed for *The Long, Long Trailer*.

Oceanfront properties were of little value to early cattle ranchers in Orange County, for they added the hazard of stray animals falling over the cliffs that bordered their unfenced grazing grounds. It took the creation of a coastal highway in the late 1920s, when this photo was taken at Salt Creek Beach, to spark the revelation that southern Orange County's beaches and ocean views had vacation potential. This Monarch Beach section of today's Dana Point remained a wide-open oceanfront with towering cliffs and sloping terrain into the 1960s; then the development of residential communities and hotels began. The chief cross street—Crown Valley Parkway—complements the royal name of Monarch Bay. S. H. Woodruff, the major 1920s developer of what is now downtown Dana Point, included bridle trails like this one throughout his community of Mediterranean-style homes.

The coastal access along Monarch Beach is Salt Creek County Park, a three-tier combination of beach, landscaped park, and recreation area. This wide sand beach borders on reliable surf. The second level echoes the 1920s bridle path, now a paved cliffside walkway extending from Monarch Bay to the Ritz-Carlton Hotel, visible on the cliff at right of center. Dogs on leashes are allowed on this path, though neither horses nor dogs can venture onto the beach below. The top level of the park is a public ocean-view expanse that matches its neighbors—the private communities of Monarch Bay and Ritz Cove. Across Pacific Coast Highway is another resort, the St. Regis, with Tuscan-style terraces, courtyards, and fountains. The banks of historic Salt Creek, which once flowed to the sea before being channeled, was also a favorite recreation spot for Native Americans, who gave it the name translated as Salt Creek.

The rock promontory that forms the Dana Point Headlands has for centuries been a navigational seamark for California gray whales. It alerts them they are approaching their winter calving grounds in Mexican lagoons after summers in Arctic seas. High tides brush the base of the Dana Point Headlands, but low tides provide a path to venture into the tide pools. North of the point is Strand Beach, a popular playground in the 1920s, when development began in this area and this picture was taken. Before that, the bluff tops were planted with dry farming crops—mostly beans, moistened by sea mist and winter rains, making irrigation unnecessary. When author Richard Henry Dana sailed into the offshore anchorage here in 1835, he was so taken by the beauty of the setting that he called it "the only romantic spot in California" in the classic book of his visit to California, *Two Years Before the Mast*. In 1884, the point was named in his honor.

Dana Point, the landmark promontory that gave the community its name, is providing the final and most challenging part of its modern coastal definition. A development complex that has been contested for decades is finally being built upon the blufftop of the point. It will consist of a hotel, private homes, a retail complex, and an extensive nature preserve with trails overlooking Dana Point Harbor and the ocean. The Dana Strand area is included in the plan. At a certain angle, the Headlands' rock face carries the profile of an Indian chief, perfectly carved by nature. History turned full circle when this, Mission San Juan Capistrano's early embarcadero—and Orange County's first port— was developed as a small-craft harbor, opening in 1971. Today it berths 2,500 private yachts, a sportfishing fleet, and guest boats from other ports. Its Ocean Institute and Doheny State Beach with its interpretive center are special attractions of Dana Point.

Traffic through Dana Point couldn't wait for the 1929 opening of the paved Pacific Coast Highway. Here, mule-drawn scrapers smooth the roadbed that would lead south into the heart of this coastal community. Two landmark buildings, among the first to be built here, are visible. On the far right is what was the Blue Lantern Fountain Lunch and Service Station. When Dana Point's first tract opened in 1924, this building at Street of the Blue Lantern was the business address of its developer, Anna Walters. It was she who named the major streets crossing the highway for the colors of ships' lanterns. At the center of this photo, where the highway divides, is the tract office of S. H. Woodruff, who bought Walters's tract and expanded the plan, hoping it would become a major resort with a harbor, a golf course, polo grounds, and a major hotel. Only the hotel foundation was completed before the national financial crash opened the 1930s, stalling construction funding.

This dramatic southbound entry into downtown Dana Point shows the highway still divided with one-way traffic south continuing down Del Prado, while the northbound section carries the Pacific Coast Highway name. The two dominant 1920s buildings have been remodeled over the years and are still in commercial use—the Blue Lantern Fountain Lunch, at right, has been a boat store, a market, a specialty vehicle center, and now an antiques and home furnishings store. At the point where the highway divides, the early Dana Point tract office is now a sports equipment center, serving residents and visitors. The foothills of the Santa Ana Mountains, which surround the city to the south, are now dotted with homes. Its isolated location, halfway between Los Angeles and San Diego, kept Dana Point a small beach-fishing spot, unknown to visitors for decades after most of Orange County was developed.

From a spot atop the Dana Point Headlands looking southeast along Capistrano Bay, the Blue Lantern gazebo (left and inset) in the 1920s was part of this wider panoramic scene. Then there was little building on the terraces that stretched along the coast. To the far right of the coastline is San Clemente, founded in 1925 and incorporated three years later. Below is what came to be called Dana Cove. Richard Dana wrote: "Compared to the plain, dull sand-beach of the rest of the coast, this grandeur was as refreshing as a great rock in a weary land." At high tide, the sand and rock beach disappeared, so nineteenth-century longboats from trading ships had to time their visits to secure a landing. At this photo's far lower right is the first pier erected there in the 1920s, popular for fishing from then on. The fence above, circling a park area, has a concrete covering scored to resemble wood.

Dana Point Harbor, seen below the cliffs, added a new dimension to this panoramic view when it opened in 1971. The *Pilgrim*, a re-creation of the Boston-based trading ship that brought the city's namesake here, is now docked in the harbor. It is an educational workshop of the Ocean Institute, which has a second tall ship and an ocean-exploring vessel on which to stage its history and science classes, as well as onshore science laboratories. The Ocean Institute hosts an annual Tall Ship Festival, when visitors can board the ships. Completion of Dana Point Harbor triggered the town's modern image as a destination resort port. It was incorporated in 1989 to include Capistrano Beach to the southeast and Monarch Beach to the northwest. The Blue Lantern gazebo (far left and inset) still stands at cliff's edge.

During the 1920s, when the first subdividing was happening on Orange County's south coast, oil heir Edward L. Doheny Jr. bought a thousand acres of beach and bluffs between Dana Point and San Clemente. He named his Spanish-style development Capistrano Beach for its proximity to the famous mission just inland. The focal point was the Capistrano Beach Club, his elegantly appointed "sand castle." Its red tile–topped tower became a navigational beacon on seacoast charts. At one point along the strand,

Doheny built a 1,200-foot wooden pier that would serve as a fishing center for forty years. Clustered around the club were guest houses, while atop the bluffs several red-tiled mansions were built. This palisades gazebo overlooked the scene below. Despite the tragic murder of Doheny in 1929 at the age of 35, the beach club was completed. The building of Doheny's dream community continued for several years. In 1930, his family gave California what became Doheny State Beach.

In this view from nearby Pines Park, the loss of the Capistrano Beach Club and the pier becomes obvious. In 1945 they were sold. The clubhouse spent time as a gambling casino, then a private beachcomber's club. When actress Jayne Mansfield attended an Orange County Press Club lunch there, someone stole her shoes; it made headlines. The 1960s brought tragedy for both community landmarks. The club was torn down to make way for a high-rise hotel, which never got off the ground. The pier was so damaged by storms, it was condemned and finally demolished. The gazebo lookout was remodeled and surrounded with a rose garden. It now stands alone at the top of Palisades Drive, which climbs from Pacific Coast Highway up to the present custom-home neighborhood. Below can be seen Capistrano Beach County Park, with a wide strand and distinctive palm trees. Visitors don't realize that the swimming pool from the old beach club lies buried in this park's sand.

The main street of San Clemente, at the southern edge of Orange County, echoes an early location in this book—El Camino Real, the road between the Spanish missions. Here it intersects the city's other main street, Avenida Del Mar. When development began in this "Spanish Village by the Sea," all buildings were required to have Spanish Colonial Revival architecture, with white stucco walls and red-tiled roofs, by directive of its founder, Ole Hanson. Some of the finest commercial specimens of that 1920s era were clustered at this intersection. On the left corner with an El Camino Real address was the Bartlett Building with Carl Romer's general store. On the right corner was San Clemente's first commercial building, the office of founder Ole Hanson. It was the San Clemente Art Shop when this photo was taken in the 1940s. Next down the Del Mar block was Travaglini's Dining Room, then the Taylor Building, then the landmark San Clemente Hotel.

This cluster of 1920s Spanish Colonial Revival buildings has been preserved and protected at the crossroads of San Clemente. The city has renovated Avenida Del Mar itself to bring back the colorful Spanish look of its early days. The Bartlett Building on the left corner became a drugstore and is now Rocky's Surf City. Ole Hanson's office across the street is now a Baskin-Robbins ice cream shop. The oldest restaurant site in town now belongs to the Gordon James Grill. The Taylor Building was long a hardware store and is now Stanford Court Antiques and Decorative Arts. The San Clemente Hotel was converted to apartments with a restaurant courtyard. Another landmark building at the head of Del Mar, off the right edge of this photo, is the historic city hall, now home of the San Clemente Historical Society and other tenants. The attractive city has long been a tourist site, attracting visitors wanting to experience the ambiance of old Spain.

As Prohibition and the Great Depression left their marks on each community, San Clemente had an answer for recovery as they ended—the opening of an elegant circular casino in 1937. Its cocktail bar served drinks legally. The highlight, though, was its circular floating ballroom, illuminated by battery-powered lights in contant motion. Since it overlooked North Beach, it featured a nautical theme and was roofed with a gigantic silver dome. It had an air-conditioning system and the latest in sound amplification. This pleasure palace was just what depression-weary dancers needed, and they came from all over Southern California. Five thousand overflowed the casino for its grand opening. It wasn't hard to find at El Camino Real and Avenida Pico, for outdoor Hollywood klieg lights announced it through the night sky and the roof sign was an invitation to "DANCE." Live radio broadcasts went out from the casino six nights a week, with big-name bands playing there regularly.

When the dancing craze died down, the casino became a private gambling hall, living up to another meaning of its "casino" name. It also did a stretch as a Moose Lodge. From the 1960s onward, it had a popular run as Sebastian's West Dinner Theatre. A year after the casino opened, the San Clemente Theatre was opened next door. Its Spanish style reflected the theme of the city—red-tiled roof, white textured plaster, and hewn wooden beams. Both buildings, still intact today, stand boldly together waiting for their next assignment. The theater has been empty for many years. The casino has in recent years served as offices for various businesses. Both distinctive buildings are currently for sale, with no indication whether they may be restored for another life or sacrificed for a different commercial use.

Though hidden from the main streets of San Clemente by a web of winding streets leading down to the sea, the San Clemente Pier has been the focus of community activity since it was built in 1928. Each of its wooden pilings was hauled individually by men and mules along those winding streets. Residents were so excited to see it finished that they gained permission to use the first nine hundred feet before the last three hundred were ready. The seaward slope of the terrain in that vicinity led to its being called the Pier Bowl.

Founder Ole Hanson had the pier built as part of his initial development, then gave it and the beach to the city when it was incorporated in 1928. The Santa Fe Railway added a stop at the pier, bringing inlanders down to share these municipal treasures. When surfing caught on, vehicles that could carry surfboards were in demand—none more than the fabled Woody station wagons like the one parked in this late-1940s photo.

Each time the San Clemente Pier has been damaged by storms, residents have willingly supported bond issues to resurrect it. They also speak out when development is proposed that might change the beach-town environment of their Pier Bowl. Some of those who have fished, surfed, or swum around this pier have been United States Marines stationed at Camp Pendleton, the vast training base just south of San Clemente. In 2005, with so many local Marines serving overseas in distant wars, the nonprofit Heritage of San Clemente Foundation designed a permanent tribute to their military neighbors who had meshed so well with the community over the years. A bronze statue was commissioned: a Marine in full dress uniform now salutes the American flag that flies over the Pier Bowl. A view park there has been dedicated to the Marines and named for the Corps' motto, Semper Fi ("always faithful").